Albert S. Cook

Poetry, with Reference to Aristotle's Poetics

Albert S. Cook

Poetry, with Reference to Aristotle's Poetics

ISBN/EAN: 9783337092078

Printed in Europe, USA, Canada, Australia, Japan

Cover: Foto ©Thomas Meinert / pixelio.de

More available books at **www.hansebooks.com**

John Henry Newman

POETRY, WITH REFERENCE TO ARISTOTLE'S POETICS

EDITED

WITH INTRODUCTION AND NOTES

BY

ALBERT S. COOK

PROFESSOR OF THE ENGLISH LANGUAGE AND LITERATURE
IN YALE UNIVERSITY

——o°⁀o⁀o°o——

BOSTON, U.S.A.
PUBLISHED BY GINN & COMPANY
1891

Typography by J. S. Cushing & Co., Boston, U.S.A.

Presswork by Ginn & Co., Boston, U.S.A.

INTRODUCTION.

NEWMAN'S essay challenges the attention of students of English on three several grounds. The first is his eminence as a stylist, the second his attempt to determine fundamental poetic principles, and the third his inclusion of ancient and modern writers in a single view.

Newman is justly celebrated as a master of lucid, copious, straightforward, vigorous prose. The simple manliness of his more popular writing contrasts favorably with the affectation and caprice of many of his contemporaries, and its qualities will never grow old, whatever may be the judgment of posterity on some of its author's opinions. Newman's mind was nourished by liberal studies, and from those studies he extracted the kernel of substance, not contenting himself with the husk of accident. From his acquaintance with language and literature he gained the ideas of a prince among men, as well as the accuracy of a grammarian. The breathing thoughts and burning words with which he became familiar, at once quickened his intelligence and enlarged its sphere, so that he became capable of reasoning both amply and subtly. His convictions, whether acceptable to others or not, and though subject to change for what he esteemed sufficient cause, were at all events based upon inquiry and meditation ; they were not the mere rags and shreds of others' thought, caught up and worn at secondhand. His definition of originality, on page 22 of the present essay, might have been framed from an inspection of the workings of his own mind. Conviction gives birth to decision, a striking quality of his prose, and it generates the power of arrangement, which he discusses on pages 26 and 27. In fact, his prose casts over the reader the spell exerted by the excellent novelist or poet. The mind is gently, yet firmly, directed into certain channels, and made to follow the course marked out for it. For the time being, one feels himself in the hands of a strong yet reasonable and beneficent master, and has neither the energy nor the desire to resist his will. It is sufficient that the superior mind is aware of the goal toward which our footsteps are guided.

There are some, who, after repeated examination of Newman's thought, will doubt its sufficiency, yet even they can not resist the impression produced by its orderly development. It is the province of all art to cheat us with gradation. The highest altitude of a bas-relief may be only some insignificant fraction of an inch, yet the spectator will persuade himself that he sees in it the natural proportions of a whole group of human forms. The setting sun of a landscape piece may be actually represented by an opaque, dull yellow, yet appear to glow with the whitest of dazzling light. The novelist's climax may be an insignificant event, which in real life would be passed by without remark, yet we shall be excited to the uttermost as we approach and reach it. Gradation deceives us with the semblance of wholes, of adequacy, of truth, of singular importance. Newman is aware of this, as he explicitly avers, and few modern writers have made a more effective use of the principle. He masses and groups particulars, the individual significance of which we can not help confessing, with reference to a generalization which seems to follow of itself, unaided by effort on our part or his. ⸱ Link by link the chain of his logic is wound about us, and before we know it we are bound hand and foot in a bondage so pleasing that we almost prefer it to liberty. Whether he deliver an address, conduct an argument, or relate a story, the result always seems predestined ; easily, insensibly, yet inevitably, the reader feels himself impelled toward a foregone conclusion. ⸱

Other marks of Newman's style there doubtless are, such as the absence of remote and passing allusion ; the sparing, but convincing, use of simile, of which there is an example on page 4 ; its stately harmony ; the mastery of language which he himself recommends, so that speech becomes the most diaphanous of veils, or rather like that clear light in which Æneas shone, when the enshrouding mist was parted and resolved itself into the colors of the sky. But it is no part of my purpose to write an essay on Newman's style; it is sufficient to feel assured that it represents something more than verbal jugglery, that it stands for art in a larger sense, that it embodies the features of a personality rather than the mere dexterities of rhetorical craftsmanship.

A second claim upon our attention arises from his inquiry into the principles which underlie great poetry. It is scarcely too much to say that the best poetry has been produced at epochs when these principles were well understood, and that they can only be perfectly understood in epochs which are capable of producing the best poetry.   The fact, therefore, that there is at present a growing interest in the investigation of the canons of poetic art is at once an augury rich with hope, and a monition to which the promptest and most cheerful obedience should be rendered.

The third reason is to be found in the catholicity of Newman's knowledge and taste.   He is not the partisan of a school or clique.   He can admire a scientist like Aristotle, or tragedians like the immortal three of Greece.   Sophocles does not blind him to the merits of Euripides, nor yet of Shakespeare.   In one breath he couples Scott and Crabbe, in another Scott and Homer, and in still another, this time for purposes of censure, Scott and Cowper.   For a certain trait he extols Bernard Barton, for another he criticises Virgil.   One who is acquainted with so wide a range of poetry, if he be, like Newman, a person of fine discernment, sound intuitions, and correct principles of reasoning, may render inestimable service to the student at almost any stage of his progress.   To the beginner he offers a method, and to the more advanced inquirer a means of rectifying partial or erroneous views ; to all a stimulus to independent reading and reflection.   It is impossible to contrast and endeavor to harmonize productions of widely sundered ages and nationalities, yet of the same general design and character, without winning in the pursuit some of the most precious rewards which culture has it in her power to bestow.

To yield the most satisfactory results, the opinions of Newman should be compared with those of other writers on the same subject, with those of Aristotle himself, of Plato, and of derivative writers like Sidney and Shelley.

But it is quite as desirable to attempt a verification of his judgments by an examination of the authors whom he cites. A useful auxiliary in the study of the Greek tragedians will be found in Moulton's *Ancient Classical Drama*, which contains a list of available translations; with Moulton's suggestive book may be compared Schlegel's *Lectures on Dramatic Art and Literature.* Translations of the complete plays of Æschylus, Sophocles, and Euripides may now be had in Morley's Universal Library (published by Routledge & Sons, London and New York, at a shilling a volume); Æschylus and Sophocles are each contained in a single volume, Euripides in three. No other English translation of Euripides is accessible; better ones of Æschylus and Sophocles are by Plumptre (published by Isbister, London, at seven shillings sixpence and four shillings sixpence respectively). Mrs. Browning has a poetical rendering of the *Prometheus Bound* of Æschylus, and Robert Browning of the *Alcestis* of Euripides, the latter under the title of *Balaustion's Adventure.* The *Iliad* may be had in the prose translation of Lang, Leaf, and Myers (Macmillan), the *Odyssey* in that of Butcher and Lang (Macmillan) or of Palmer (Houghton, Mifflin & Co.); besides these, the poetical translation of both epics by Bryant (Houghton, Mifflin & Co., each volume $2.50), and that of the *Odyssey* by Worsley (Blackwood, Edinburgh and London, twelve shillings) are to be recommended. There is an English translation of Aristotle's *Poetics* by Wharton, with the Greek on opposite pages (Parker, Oxford and London, two shillings and sixpence), and one by Twining in Cassell's National Library, without the Greek, but in the same volume with Longinus

On the Sublime, for ten cents. With the works men-
tioned, and the English authors referred to by Newman,
a teacher of literature ought to have no difficulty in
framing an attractive and profitable course in poetry
and imaginative writing ; nor would it be time thrown
away to read the essay of Newman by itself.

ANALYSIS.

————•◦•————

Announcement of subject, 1 1–3.

I. Whether plot is of chief importance in tragedy, 1 4—9 23.
    A. The Greek tragedies do not confirm Aristotle's theory of plot, 1 4—8 3.
        1. Illustration from the *Agamemnon* of Æschylus, the *Œdipus Tyrannus* of Sophocles, and the *Bacchæ* of Euripides, 5 8—8 3.
    B. Discussion of Aristotle's error, 8 4—9 23, and transition to next head 9 24–8.

II. Poetry a representation of the ideal, 9 29—21 25.
    A. Beauty and perfection the standard of poetry, 9 29—12 27.
        1. This differentiates poetry from history and biography, 9 29—10 27.
        2. For the same reason it naturally allies itself with metaphor and music, 10 28—11 20.
        3. Portions of otherwise great poems may be unpoetical, 11 21—12 27.
    B. Poetic idealization considered with reference to its subjects, 12 28—21 25.
        1. Description idealized, 12 29—13 32.
            a. Description unidealized : Empedocles, Oppian, Thomson (?), 12 29—13 12.
            b. Description properly idealized : Milton, 13 12-20.
            c. Description over-idealized : Virgil and Pope, 13 20-28.
        2. Narrative idealized, 14 1—15 8.
            a. Narrative unidealized : Horace Smith's *Brambletye House;* and idealized : Scott's *Peveril of the Peak,* 14 21-28.
            b. Anomalous experiences unavailable for poetry, 14 28—15 8.

3. Character idealized, 15 9—17 27.
    a. Circumstances under which idealization is unnecessary, 15 30—16 11.
    b. Idealization consistent with individualization, 16 12—23.
    c. And with the introduction of imperfect or odious characters, 16 23—17 6.
    d. The satisfaction of poetic justice *may* be referred to a future life, 17 6—26.

4. Opinions, feelings, manners, and customs idealized, 17 28—19 24.
    a. Especially in the ode, elegy, sonnet, and ballad, 17 30—18 16.
    b. But also in didactic and moralizing poems, 18 17—19 24.
        aa. But declamation and poetry are here often confounded, though directly opposite in nature, 18 21—19 24.

5. The philosophy of mind idealized, 19 25—21 25.
    a. Delicate characterization in Crabbe and Scott, 20 4—21 1.
    b. Lack of it in Byron, 21 1—22.

III. Relation of originality to poetic talent, 21 27—25 19.
  A. Poetic talent the originality of right moral feeling, 22 1—3.
  B. Definition of originality, 22 4—18.
  C. Poetry the originality of grace, refinement, purity, and good feeling, 22 18—29.
    1. Whether this doctrine is confirmed by experience, 22 30—23 24.
    2. Poets who exhibit correct moral perception, 23 24—24 1.
    3. Some who are deficient in it, 24 1—24.
  D. The poetry in religion, 24 25—25 19.

IV. Poetical composition, 25 20—28 19.
  A. The art of composition merely accessory to the poetical talent, 25 21—22.
  B. Causes of obscurity in poetical writings, 25 24—26 9.
  C. Poetical eloquence, 26 10—27 16.
    1. Power of illustration, 26 14—20.
    2. Power of arrangement, 26 20—27 4.
    3. Command of language, 27 4—16.
  D. Attention to language for its own sake to be deprecated, 27 17—31.
  E. Examples of adequacy, inadequacy, and affectation of style, 27 32—28 19.

V. Note on the definition of poetry : Poetry the gift of moving the affections through the imagination, and its object the beautiful, 29.

POETRY, WITH REFERENCE TO
ARISTOTLE'S POETICS.

WE propose to offer some speculations of our own
on Greek Tragedy, and on Poetry in general, as
suggested by the doctrine of Aristotle on the subject.

I.

Aristotle considers the excellence of a tragedy to
depend upon its plot — and, since a tragedy, as such, is ₅
obviously the exhibition of an action, no one can deny
his statement to be abstractedly true. Accordingly he
directs his principal attention to the economy of the
fable; determines its range of subjects, delineates its
proportions, traces its progress from a complication of ₁₀
incidents to their just and satisfactory settlement, in-
vestigates the means of making a train of events striking
or affecting, and shows how the exhibition of character
may be made subservient to the purpose of the action.
His treatise is throughout interesting and valuable. It ₁₅
is one thing, however, to form the *beau idéal* of a tragedy
on scientific principles; another to point out the actual
beauty of a particular school of dramatic composition.
The Greek tragedians are not generally felicitous in the
construction of their plots. Aristotle, then, rather tells ₂₀
us what Tragedy should be, than what Greek Tragedy

really was.   And this doubtless was the intention of the
philosopher.   Since, however, the Greek drama has
obtained so extended and lasting a celebrity, and yet
its excellence does not fall under the strict rules of the
5 critical art, we have to inquire in what it consists.

That the charm of Greek Tragedy does not ordinarily
arise from scientific correctness of plot, is certain as a
matter of fact. ⌈Seldom does any great interest arise
from the action ; which, instead of being progressive and
10 sustained, is commonly either a mere necessary condition
of the drama, or a convenience for the introduction of
matter more important than itself.⌉ It is often stationary
— often irregular — sometimes either wants or outlives
the catastrophe.   In the plays of Æschylus it is always
15 simple and inartificial ; in four out of the seven there is
hardly any plot at all ; and though it is of more prom-
inent importance in those of Sophocles, yet even here
the Œdipus at Colonus is a mere series of incidents, and
the Ajax a union of two separate subjects ; while in the
20 Philoctetes, which is apparently busy, the circumstances
of the action are but slightly connected with the *dénoue-
ment.*   The carelessness of Euripides in the construction of his plots is well known.   The action then will
be more justly viewed as the vehicle for introducing the
25 personages of the drama, than as the principal object of
the poet's art ; it is not in the plot, but in the characters, sentiments, and diction, that the actual merit and
poetry of the composition are found.   To show this to
the satisfaction of the reader would require a minuter
30 investigation of details than our present purpose admits ;
yet a few instances in point may suggest others to the
memory.

For instance, in neither the Œdipus Coloneus nor the Philoctetes, the two most beautiful plays of Sophocles, is the plot striking ; but how exquisite is the delineation of the characters of Antigone and Œdipus, in the former tragedy, particularly in their interview with Polynices, 5 and the various descriptions of the scene itself which the Chorus furnishes ! In the Philoctetes, again, it is the contrast between the worldly wisdom of Ulysses, the inexperienced frankness of Neoptolemus, and the simplicity of the afflicted Philoctetes, which constitutes the 10 principal charm of the drama. Or we may instance the spirit and nature displayed in the grouping of the characters in the Prometheus, which is almost without action ; the stubborn enemy of the new dynasty of gods ; Oceanus trimming, as an accomplished politician, with 15 the change of affairs ; the single-hearted and generous Nereids ; and Hermes, the favorite and instrument of the usurping potentate. So again, the beauties of the Thebæ are almost independent of the plot ; it is the Chorus which imparts grace and interest to the action- 20 less scene ; and the speech of Antigone at the end, one of the most simply striking in any play, has, scientifically speaking, no place in the tragedy, which should already have been brought to its conclusion. Then again, amid the multitude of the beauties of the irreg- 25 ular Euripides, it would be obvious to notice the character of Alcestis, and of Clytemnestra in the Electra ; the soliloquies of Medea ; the picturesque situation of Ion, the minister of the Pythian temple ; the opening scene of the Orestes ; and the dialogues between Phædra 30 and her attendant in the Hippolytus, and the old man and Antigone in the Phœnissæ ; — passages nevertheless which are either unconnected with the development of the plot, or of an importance superior to it.

Thus the Greek drama, as a fact, was modeled on no scientific principle. It was a pure recreation of the imagination, reveling without object or meaning beyond its own exhibition. Gods, heroes, kings, and dames, enter and retire : they may have a good reason for appearing, — they may have a very poor one ; whatever it is, still we have no right to ask for it ; the question is impertinent. Let us listen to their harmonious and majestic language, to the voices of sorrow, joy, compassion, or religious emotion, — to the animated odes of the chorus. Why interrupt so transcendent a display of poetical genius by inquiries degrading it to the level of every-day events, and implying incompleteness in the action till a catastrophe arrives ? The very spirit of beauty breathes through every part of the composition. We may liken the Greek drama to the music of the Italian school ; in which the wonder is, how so much richness of invention in detail can be accommodated to a style so simple and uniform. Each is the development of grace, fancy, pathos, and taste, in the respective media of representation and sound.

However true then it may be that one or two of the most celebrated dramas answer to the requisitions of Aristotle's doctrine, still, for the most part, Greek Tragedy has its own distinct and peculiar praise, which must not be lessened by a criticism conducted on principles, whether correct or not, still leading to excellence of another character. This being as we hope shown, we shall be still bolder, and proceed to question even the sufficiency of the rules of Aristotle for the production of dramas of the highest order. These rules, it would appear, require a fable not merely natural and unaffected, as a vehicle of more poetical matter, but one labored and complicated, as the sole legitimate channel of tragic effect ; and thus tend to withdraw the mind of the poet from the spontaneous exhibition of pathos or imagination to a minute diligence in the formation of a plot.

2.

To explain our views on the subject, we will institute a short comparison between three tragedies, the Agamemnon, the Œdipus, and the Bacchæ, one of each of the tragic poets, as to which, by reference to Aristotle's principles, we think it will be found that the most perfect in plot is not the most poetical.

1. Of these, the action of the Œdipus Tyrannus is frequently instanced by the critic as a specimen of judgment and skill in the selection and combination of the incidents ; and in this point of view it is truly a masterly composition. The clearness, precision, certainty, and vigor with which the line of the action moves on to its termination is admirable. The character of Œdipus, too, is finely drawn, and identified with the development of the action.

2. The Agamemnon of Æschylus presents us with the slow and difficult birth of a portentous secret — an event of old written in the resolves of destiny, a crime long meditated in the bosom of the human agents. The Chorus here has an importance altogether wanting in the Chorus of the Œdipus. They throw a pall of ancestral honor over the bier of the hereditary monarch,

which would have been unbecoming in the case of the upstart king of Thebes.   Till the arrival of Agamemnon they occupy our attention, as the prophetic organ, not commissioned indeed, but employed by heaven, to proclaim the impending horrors.   Succeeding to the brief intimation of the watcher who opens the play, they seem oppressed with forebodings of woe and crime which they can neither justify nor analyze.   The expression of their anxiety forms the stream in which the plot flows — everything, even news of joy, takes a coloring from the depth of their gloom.   On the arrival of the king, they retire before Cassandra, a more regularly commissioned prophetess ; who, speaking first in figure, then in plain terms, only ceases that we may hear the voice of the betrayed monarch himself, informing us of the striking of the fatal blow.   Here, then, the very simplicity of the fable constitutes its especial beauty.   The death of Agamemnon is intimated at first — it is accomplished at last ; throughout we find but the growing in volume and intensity of one and the same note — it is a working up of one musical ground, by figure and imitation, into the richness of combined harmony.   But we look in vain for the progressive and thickening incidents of the Œdipus.

3. The action of the Bacchæ is also simple.   It is the history of the reception of the worship of Bacchus in Thebes ; who, first depriving Pentheus of his reason, and thereby drawing him on to his ruin, reveals his own divinity.   The interest of the scene arises from the gradual process by which the derangement of the Theban king is effected, which is powerfully and originally described.   It would be comic, were it unconnected with

religion. As it is, it exhibits the grave irony of a god triumphing over the impotent presumption of man, the sport and terrible mischievousness of an insulted deity. It is an exemplification of the adage, "Quem deus vult perdere, prius dementat." So delicately balanced is the 5 action along the verge of the sublime and grotesque, that it is both solemn and humorous, without violence to the propriety of the composition : the mad fire of the Chorus, the imbecile mirth of old Cadmus and Tiresias, and the infatuation of Pentheus, who is ultimately in- 10 duced to dress himself in female garb to gain admittance among the Bacchæ, are made to harmonize with the terrible catastrophe which concludes the life of the intruder. Perhaps the victim's first discovery of the disguised deity is the finest conception in this splendid 15 drama. His madness enables him to discern the emblematic horns on the head of Bacchus, which were hid from him when in his sound mind ; yet this discovery, instead of leading him to an acknowledgment of the divinity, provides him only with matter for a stupid and 20 perplexed astonishment :

> A Bull, thou seem'st to lead us ; on thy head
> Horns have grown forth : wast heretofore a beast?
> For such thy semblance now.

This play is on the whole the most favorable speci- 25 men of the genius of Euripides — not breathing the sweet composure, the melodious fulness, the majesty and grace of Sophocles ; nor rudely and overpoweringly tragic as Æschylus ; but brilliant, versatile, imaginative, as well as deeply pathetic. Here then are two dramas 30 of extreme poetical power, but deficient in skilfulness of

plot.   Are they on that account to be rated below the
Œdipus, which, in spite of its many beauties, has not
even a share of the richness and sublimity of either?

3.

Aristotle, then, it must be allowed, treats dramatic
5 composition more as an exhibition of ingenious work-
manship than as a free and unfettered effusion of
genius.   The inferior poem may, on his principle, be
the better tragedy.   He may indeed have intended
solely to delineate the outward framework most suit-
10 able to the reception of the spirit of poetry, not to dis-
cuss the nature of poetry itself.   If so, it cannot be
denied that, the poetry being given equal in the two
cases, the more perfect plot will merit the greater share
of praise.   And it may seem to agree with this view of
15 his meaning, that he pronounces Euripides, in spite of
the irregularity of his plots, to be after all the most
tragic of the Greek dramatists, that is, inasmuch as he
excels in his appeal to those passions which the outward
form of the drama merely subserves.   Still there is
20 surely too much stress laid by the philosopher upon the
artificial part ; which, after all, leads to negative more
than to positive excellence ; and should rather be the
natural and, so to say, unintentional result of the poet's
feeling and imagination, than be separated from them
25 as the direct object of his care.   Perhaps it is hardly
fair to judge of Aristotle's sentiments by the fragment
of his work which has come down to us.   Yet as his
natural taste led him to delight in the explication of
systems, and in those connected views following upon

his vigorous talent for thinking through large subjects, we may be allowed to suspect him of entertaining too cold and formal conceptions of the nature of poetical composition, as if its beauties were less subtile and delicate than they really are. A word has power to convey a world of information to the imagination, and to act as a spell upon the feelings ; there is no need of sustained fiction, — often no room for it. The sudden inspiration, surely, of the blind Œdipus, in the second play bearing his name, by which he is enabled, "without a guide," to lead the way to his place of death, in our judgment produces more poetical effect than all the skilful intricacy of the plot of the Tyrannus. The latter excites an interest which scarcely lasts beyond the first reading — the former "decies repetita placebit."

Some confirmation of the judgment we have ventured to pass on the greatest of analytical philosophers is the account he gives of the source of poetical pleasure ; which he almost identifies with a gratification of the reasoning faculty, placing it in the satisfaction derived from recognizing in fiction a resemblance to the realities of life — "The spectators are led to recognize and to syllogize what each thing is."

But as we have treated, rather unceremoniously, a deservedly high authority, we will try to compensate for our rudeness by illustrating his general doctrine of the nature of Poetry, which we hold to be most true and philosophical.

4.

Poetry, according to Aristotle, is a representation of the ideal. Biography and history represent individual

characters and actual facts ; poetry, on the contrary, generalizing from the phenomenon of nature and life, supplies us with pictures drawn, not after an existing pattern, but after a creation of the mind. Fidelity is
5 the primary merit of biography and history ; the essence of poetry is fiction." " Poesis nihil aliud est," says Bacon, " quam historiæ imitatio ad placitum." It delineates that perfection which the imagination suggests, and to which as a limit the present system of Divine Provi-
10 dence actually tends. Moreover, by confining the attention to one series of events and scene of action, it bounds and finishes off the confused luxuriance of real nature ; while, by a skilful adjustment of circumstances, it brings into sight the connexion of cause and effect,
15 completes the dependence of the parts one on another, and harmonizes the proportions of the whole. It is then but the type and model of history or biography, if we may be allowed the comparison, bearing some resemblance to the abstract mathematical formulæ of physics,
20 before they are modified by the contingencies of atmosphere and friction. ' Hence, while it recreates the imagination by the superhuman loveliness of its views, it provides a solace for the mind broken by the disappointments and sufferings of actual life ; and becomes, more-
25 over, the utterance of the inward emotions of a right moral feeling, seeking a purity and a truth which this world will not give.

It follows that the poetical mind is one full of the eternal forms of beauty and perfection ; these are its
30 material of thought, its instrument and medium of observation, — these color each object to which it directs its view. It is called imaginative or creative from the

originality and independence of its modes of thinking,
compared with the commonplace and matter-of-fact conceptions of ordinary minds, which are fettered down to
the particular and individual. At the same time it feels
a natural sympathy with everything great and splendid 5
in the physical and moral world ; and selecting such from
the mass of common phenomena, incorporates them, as
it were, into the substance of its own creations. From
living thus in a world of its own, it speaks the language
of dignity, emotion, and refinement. Figure is its neces- 10
sary medium of communication with man ; for in the
feebleness of ordinary words to express its ideas, and in
the absence of terms of abstract perfection, the adoption
of metaphorical language is the only poor means allowed
it for imparting to others its intense feelings. A met- 15
rical garb has, in all languages, been appropriated to
poetry — it is but the outward development of the music
and harmony within. The verse, far from being a re-
straint on the true poet, is the suitable index of his
sense, and is adopted by his free and deliberate choice. 20
We shall presently show the applicability of our doctrine
to the various departments of poetical composition ; first,
however, it will be right to volunteer an explanation
which may save it from much misconception and objec-
tion. Let not our notion be thought arbitrarily to limit 25
the number of poets, generally considered such. It will
be found to lower particular works, or parts of works,
rather than the authors themselves ; sometimes to dis-
parage only the vehicle in which the poetry is conveyed.
There is an ambiguity in the word "poetry," which is 30
taken to signify both the gift itself, and the written
composition which is the result of it. Thus there is an

apparent, but no real contradiction, in saying a poem may be but partially poetical; in some passages more so than in others; and sometimes not poetical at all. We only maintain, not that the writers forfeit the name
5 of poet who fail at times to answer to our requisitions, but that they are poets only so far forth, and inasmuch as they do answer to them. We may grant, for instance, that the vulgarities of old Phœnix in the ninth Iliad, or of the nurse of Orestes in the Chœphorœ, are in them-
10 selves unworthy of their respective authors, and refer them to the wantonness of exuberant genius ; and yet maintain that the scenes in question contain much incidental poetry. Now and then the lustre of the true metal catches the eye, redeeming whatever is unseemly
15 and worthless in the rude ore ; still the ore is not the metal. Nay, sometimes, and not unfrequently in Shakspeare, the introduction of unpoetical matter may be necessary for the sake of relief, or as a vivid expression of recondite conceptions, and, as it were, to make friends
20 with the reader's imagination. This necessity, however, cannot make the additions in themselves beautiful and pleasing. Sometimes, on the other hand, while we do not deny the incidental beauty of a poem, we are ashamed and indignant on witnessing the unworthy
25 substance in which that beauty is imbedded. This remark applies strongly to the immoral compositions to which Lord Byron devoted his last years.

5.

Now to proceed with our proposed investigation.
1. We will notice *descriptive poetry* first. Empedocles

wrote his physics in verse, and Oppian his history of animals. Neither were poets — the one was an historian of nature, the other a sort of biographer of brutes. Yet a poet may make natural history or philosophy the material of his composition. But under his hands they 5 are no longer a bare collection of facts or principles, but are painted with a meaning, beauty, and harmonious order not their own. Thomson has sometimes been commended for the novelty and minuteness of his remarks upon nature. This is not the praise of a poet; 10 whose office rather is to represent known phenomena in a new connexion or medium. In L'Allegro and Il Penseroso the poetical magician invests the commonest scenes of a country life with the hues, first of a cheerful, then of a pensive imagination. It is the charm of 15 the descriptive poetry of a religious mind that nature is viewed in a moral connexion. Ordinary writers, for instance, compare aged men to trees in autumn — a gifted poet will in the fading trees discern the fading men.* Pastoral poetry is a description of rustics, agri- 20 culture, and cattle, softened off and corrected from the rude health of nature. Virgil, and much more Pope and others, have run into the fault of coloring too highly; instead of drawing generalized and ideal forms of shepherds, they have given us pictures of gentlemen 25 and beaux.

Their composition may be poetry, but it is not pastoral poetry.

* Thus:— "How quiet shows the woodland scene!
　　　Each flower and tree, its duty done, 30
　　　Reposing in decay serene,
　　　Like weary men when age is won," etc.

2. The difference between poetical and historical *narrative* may be illustrated by the Tales Founded on Facts, generally of a religious character, so common in the present day, which we must not be thought to approve
5 because we use them for our purpose. The author finds in the circumstances of the case many particulars too trivial for public notice, or irrelevant to the main story, or partaking perhaps too much of the peculiarity of individual minds: these he omits. He finds connected
10 events separated from each other by time or place, or a course of action distributed among a multitude of agents ; he limits the scene or duration of the tale, and dispenses with his host of characters by condensing the mass of incident and action in the history of a few. He
15 compresses long controversies into a concise argument, and exhibits characters by dialogue, and (if such be his object) brings prominently forward the course of Divine Providence by a fit disposition of his materials. Thus he selects, combines, refines, colors, — in fact, poetizes.
20 His facts are no longer actual, but ideal ; a tale founded on facts is a tale generalized from facts. The authors of Peveril of the Peak, and of Brambletye House, have given us their respective descriptions of the profligate times of Charles II. Both accounts are interesting, but
25 for different reasons. That of the latter writer has the fidelity of history ; Walter Scott's picture is the hideous reality unintentionally softened and decorated by the poetry of his own mind. Miss Edgeworth sometimes apologizes for certain incidents in her tales by stating
30 they took place "by one of those strange chances which occur in life, but seem incredible when found in writing." Such an excuse evinces a misconception of the

principle of fiction, which, being the perfection of the actual, prohibits the introduction of any such anomalies of experience. It is by a similar impropriety that painters sometimes introduce unusual sunsets, or other singular phenomena of lights and forms. Yet some of Miss Edgeworth's works contain much poetry of narrative. Manœuvring is perfect in its way, — the plot and characters are natural, without being too real to be pleasing.

3. *Character* is made poetical by a like process. The writer draws indeed from experience; but unnatural peculiarities are laid aside, and harsh contrasts reconciled. If it be said, the fidelity of the imitation is often its greatest merit, we have only to reply that in such cases the pleasure is not poetical, but consists in the mere recognition. All novels and tales which introduce real characters are in the same degree unpoetical. Portrait-painting, to be poetical, should furnish an abstract representation of an individual; the abstraction being more rigid, inasmuch as the painting is confined to one point of time. The artist should draw independently of the accidents of attitude, dress, occasional feeling, and transient action. He should depict the general spirit of his subject — as if he were copying from memory, not from a few particular sittings. An ordinary painter will delineate with rigid fidelity, and will make a caricature; but the learned artist contrives so to temper his composition as to sink all offensive peculiarities and hardnesses of individuality, without diminishing the striking effect of the likeness, or acquainting the casual spectator with the secret of his art. Miss Edgeworth's representations of the Irish character are actual, and not poetical — nor were they intended to be so. They

are interesting, because they are faithful. If there is
poetry about them, it exists in the personages themselves, not in her representation of them. She is only
the accurate reporter in word of what was poetical in
5 fact.   Hence, moreover, when a deed or incident is
striking in itself, a judicious writer is led to describe it
in the most simple and colorless terms, his own being
unnecessary ; for instance, if the greatness of the action
itself excites the imagination, or the depth of the suffer-
10 ing interests the feelings.   In the usual phrase, the circumstances are left "to speak for themselves."

Let it not be said that our doctrine is adverse to that
individuality in the delineation of character which is a
principal charm of fiction.   It is not necessary for the
15 ideality of a composition to avoid those minuter shades
of difference between man and man which give to
poetry its plausibility and life ; but merely such viola-
tion of general nature, such improbabilities, wanderings,
or coarsenesses, as interfere with the refined and deli-
20 cate enjoyment of the imagination ; which would have
the elements of beauty extracted out of the confused
multitude of ordinary actions and habits, and combined
with consistency and ease.   Nor does it exclude the
introduction of imperfect or odious characters.   The
25 original conception of a weak or guilty mind may have
its intrinsic beauty ; and much more so, when it is connected with a tale which finally adjusts whatever is
reprehensible in the personages themselves.   Richard
and Iago are subservient to the plot.   Moral excellence
30 in some characters may become even a fault.   The Clytemnestra of Euripides is so interesting that the divine
vengeance, which is the main subject of the drama,

seems almost unjust. Lady Macbeth, on the contrary, is the conception of one deeply learned in the poetical art. She is polluted with the most heinous crimes, and meets the fate she deserves. Yet there is nothing in the picture to offend the taste, and much to feed the 5 imagination. Romeo and Juliet are too good for the termination to which the plot leads; so are Ophelia and the Bride of Lammermoor. In these cases there is something inconsistent with correct beauty, and there- fore unpoetical. We do not say the fault could be 10 avoided without sacrificing more than would be gained; still it is a fault. It is scarcely possible for a poet satisfactorily to connect innocence with ultimate unhap- piness, when the notion of a future life is excluded. Honors paid to the memory of the dead are some 15 alleviation of the harshness. In his use of the doctrine of a future life, Southey is admirable. Other writers are content to conduct their heroes to temporal happi- ness;—Southey refuses present comfort to his Ladur- lad, Thalaba, and Roderick, but carries them on through 20 suffering to another world. The death of his hero is the termination of the action; yet so little in two of them, at least, does this catastrophe excite sorrowful feelings, that some readers may be startled to be re- minded of the fact. If a melancholy is thrown over the 25 conclusion of the Roderick, it is from the peculiarities of the hero's previous history.

4. Opinions, feelings, manners, and customs, are made poetical by the delicacy or splendor with which they are expressed. This is seen in the *ode, elegy, sonnet,* and 30 *ballad;* in which a single idea, perhaps, or familiar oc- currence, is invested by the poet with pathos or dignity.

The ballad of Old Robin Gray will serve for an instance,
out of a multitude ; again, Lord Byron's Hebrew Melody,
beginning, "Were my bosom as false," etc. ; or Cowper's
Lines on his Mother's Picture ; or Milman's Funeral
5 Hymn in the Martyr of Antioch ; or Milton's Sonnet on
his Blindness ; or Bernard Barton's Dream.   As picturesque specimens, we may name Campbell's Battle of the
Baltic ; or Joanna Baillie's Chough and Crow ; and for
the more exalted and splendid style, Gray's Bard ; or Mil-
10 ton's Hymn on the Nativity ; in which facts, with which
every one is familiar, are made new by the coloring of
a poetical imagination.   It must all along be observed
that we are not adducing instances for their own sake ;
but in order to illustrate our general doctrine, and to
15 show its applicability to those compositions which are,
by universal consent, acknowledged to be poetical.

The department of poetry we are now speaking of is
of much wider extent than might at first sight appear.
It will include such moralizing and philosophical poems
20 as Young's Night Thoughts and Byron's Childe Harold.
There is much bad taste, at present, in the judgment
passed on compositions of this kind.   It is the fault of
the day to mistake mere eloquence for poetry ; whereas,
in direct opposition to the conciseness and simplicity of
25 the poet, the talent of the orator consists in making
much of a single idea.   "Sic dicet ille ut verset sæpe
multis modis eandem et unam rem, ut hæreat in eâdem
commoreturque sententiâ."   This is the great art of
Cicero himself, who, whether he is engaged in state-
30 ment, argument, or raillery, never ceases till he has ex-
hausted the subject ; going round about it, and placing
it in every different light, yet without repetition to

offend or weary the reader. This faculty seems to consist in the power of throwing off harmonious verses,
which, while they have a respectable portion of meaning, yet are especially intended to charm the ear. In
popular poems, common ideas are unfolded with copi- 5
ousness, and set off in polished verse — and this is called
poetry. Such is the character of Campbell's Pleasures
of Hope; it is in his minor poems that the author's
poetical genius rises to its natural elevation. In Childe
Harold, too, the writer is carried through his Spenserian 10
stanza with the unweariness and equable fulness of accomplished eloquence; opening, illustrating, and height-
ening one idea, before he passes on to another. His
composition is an extended funeral sermon over buried
joys and pleasures. His laments over Greece, Rome, 15
and the fallen in various engagements, have quite the
character of panegyrical orations; while by the very
attempt to describe the celebrated buildings and sculp-
tures of antiquity, he seems to confess that *they* are the
poetical text, his the rhetorical comment. Still it is a 20
work of splendid talent, though, as a whole, not of the
highest poetical excellence. Juvenal is perhaps the only
ancient author who habitually substitutes declamation
for poetry.

5. The *philosophy of mind* may equally be made sub- 25
servient to poetry, as the philosophy of nature. It is a
common fault to mistake a mere knowledge of the heart
for poetical talent. Our greatest masters have known
better; — they have subjected metaphysics to their art.
In Hamlet, Macbeth, Richard, and Othello, the philoso- 30
phy of mind is but the material of the poet. These
personages are ideal; they are effects of the contact of

a given internal character with given outward circumstances, the results of combined conditions determining (so to say) a moral curve of original and inimitable properties.   Philosophy is exhibited in the same sub-
5 serviency to poetry in many parts of Crabbe's Tales of the Hall.   In the writings of this author there is much to offend a refined taste; but, at least in the work in question, there is much of a highly poetical cast.   It is a representation of the action and reaction of two minds
10 upon each other and upon the world around them. Two brothers of different characters and fortunes, and strangers to each other, meet.   Their habits of mind, the formation of those habits by external circumstances, their respective media of judgment, their points of mu-
15 tual attraction and repulsion, the mental position of each in relation to a variety of trifling phenomena of every-day nature and life, are beautifully developed in a series of tales moulded into a connected narrative.   We are tempted to single out the fourth book, which gives an
20 account of the childhood and education of the younger brother, and which for variety of thought as well as fidelity of description is in our judgment beyond praise. The Waverley Novels would afford us specimens of a similar excellence.   One striking peculiarity of these
25 tales is the author's practice of describing a group of characters bearing the same general features of mind, and placed in the same general circumstances ; yet so contrasted with each other in minute differences of mental constitution, that each diverges from the com-
30 mon starting-point into a path peculiar to himself.   The brotherhood of villains in Kenilworth, of knights in Ivanhoe, and of enthusiasts in Old Mortality, are in-

stances of this. This bearing of character and plot on each other is not often found in Byron's poems. The Corsair is intended for a remarkable personage. We pass by the inconsistencies of his character, considered by itself. The grand fault is that, whether it be natural 5 or not, we are obliged to accept the author's word for the fidelity of his portrait. We are told, not shown, what the hero was. There is nothing in the plot which results from his peculiar formation of mind. An every-day bravo might equally well have satisfied the require- 10 ments of the action. Childe Harold, again, if he is any-thing, is a being professedly isolated from the world, and uninfluenced by it. One might as well draw Tityrus's stags grazing in the air, as a character of this kind; which yet, with more or less alteration, passes through 15 successive editions in his other poems. Byron had very little versatility or elasticity of genius; he did not know how to make poetry out of existing materials. He de-claims in his own way, and has the upperhand as long as he is allowed to go on; but, if interrogated on prin- 20 ciples of nature and good sense, he is at once put out and brought to a stand.

Yet his conception of Sardanapalus and Myrrha is fine and ideal, and in the style of excellence which we have just been admiring in Shakspeare and Scott. 25

6.

These illustrations of Aristotle's doctrine may suffice.

Now let us proceed to a fresh position; which, as be-fore, shall first be broadly stated, then modified and ex-plained. How does originality differ from the poetical

talent ? Without affecting the accuracy of a definition,
we may call the latter the originality of right moral
feeling.

Originality may perhaps be defined the power of ab-
stracting for one's self, and is in thought what strength
of mind is in action.   Our opinions are commonly derived from education and society.   Common minds trans-
mit as they receive, good and bad, true and false ; minds
of original talent feel a continual propensity to investi-
gate subjects and strike out views for themselves ; — so
that even old and established truths do not escape modification and accidental change when subjected to this
process of mental digestion.   Even the style of original
writers is stamped with the peculiarities of their minds.
When originality is found apart from good sense, which
more or less is frequently the case, it shows itself in
paradox and rashness of sentiment, and eccentricity of
outward conduct.   Poetry, on the other hand, cannot be
separated from its good sense, or taste, as it is called ;
which is one of its elements.   It is originality energiz-
ing in the world of beauty ; the originality of grace,
purity, refinement, and good feeling.   We do not hesi-
tate to say that poetry is ultimately founded on correct
moral perception ; that where there is no sound principle
in exercise there will be no poetry ; and that on the
whole (originality being granted) in proportion to the
standard of a writer's moral character will his compositions vary in poetical excellence.   This position, however, requires some explanation.

Of course, then, we do not mean to imply that a poet
must necessarily display virtuous and religious feeling ;
we are not speaking of the actual material of poetry,

but of its sources. A right moral state of heart is the formal and scientific condition of a poetical mind. Nor does it follow from our position that every poet must in fact be a man of consistent and practical principle ; except so far as good feeling commonly produces or results 5 from good practice. Burns was a man of inconsistent life ; still, it is known, of much really sound principle at bottom. Thus his acknowledged poetical talent is in nowise inconsistent with the truth of our doctrine, which will refer the beauty which exists in his compositions to 10 the remains of a virtuous and diviner nature within him. Nay, further than this, our theory holds good, even though it be shown that a depraved man may write a poem. As motives short of the purest lead to actions intrinsically good, so frames of mind short of virtuous 15 will produce a partial and limited poetry. But even where this is instanced, the poetry of a vicious mind will be inconsistent and debased; that is, so far only poetry as the traces and shadows of holy truth still remain upon it. On the other hand, a right moral feeling 20 places the mind in the very centre of that circle from which all the rays have their origin and range ; whereas minds otherwise placed command but a portion of the whole circuit of poetry. Allowing for human infirmity and the varieties of opinion, Milton, Spenser, Cowper, 25 Wordsworth, and Southey may be considered, as far as their writings go, to approximate to this moral centre. The following are added as further illustrations of our meaning. Walter Scott's centre is chivalrous honor; Shakspeare exhibits the characteristics of an unlearned 30 and undisciplined piety ; Homer the religion of nature and conscience, at times debased by polytheism. All

these poets are religious.   The occasional irreligion of Virgil's poetry is painful to the admirers of his general taste and delicacy. Dryden's Alexander's Feast is a magnificent composition, and has high poetical beauties ;
5 but to a refined judgment there is something intrinsically unpoetical in the end to which it is devoted, the praises of revel and sensuality.   It corresponds to a process of clever reasoning erected on an untrue foundation — the one is a fallacy, the other is out of taste.
10 Lord Byron's Manfred is in parts intensely poetical ; yet the delicate mind naturally shrinks from the spirit which here and there reveals itself, and the basis on which the drama is built.   From a perusal of it we should infer, according to the above theory, that there was right
15 and fine feeling in the poet's mind, but that the central and consistent character was wanting.   From the history of his life we know this to be the fact.   The connexion between want of the religious principle and want of poetical feeling is seen in the instances of Hume and
20 Gibbon, who had radically unpoetical minds.   Rousseau, it may be supposed, is an exception to our doctrine. Lucretius, too, had great poetical genius ; but his work evinces that his miserable philosophy was rather the result of a bewildered judgment than a corrupt heart.
25   According to the above theory, Revealed Religion should be especially poetical — and it is so in fact.   While its disclosures have an originality in them to engage the intellect, they have a beauty to satisfy the moral nature. It presents us with those ideal forms of excellence in
30 which a poetical mind delights, and with which all grace and harmony are associated.   It brings us into a new world — a world of overpowering interest, of the sub-

limest views and the tenderest and purest feelings. The
peculiar grace of mind of the New Testament writers is
as striking as the actual effect produced upon the hearts
of those who have imbibed their spirit. At present we
are not concerned with the practical, but the poetical, 5
nature of revealed truth. ′With Christians, a poetical
view of things is a duty, — we are bid to color all things
with hues of faith, to see a Divine meaning in every event,
and a superhuman tendency.′ Even our friends around
are invested with unearthly brightness — no longer 10
imperfect men, but beings taken into Divine favor,
stamped with His seal, and in training for future happiness. It may be added that the virtues peculiarly
Christian are especially poetical — meekness, gentleness,
compassion, contentment, modesty, not to mention the 15
devotional virtues ; whereas the ruder and more ordinary
feelings are the instruments of rhetoric more justly than
of poetry — anger, indignation, emulation, martial spirit,
and love of independence.′

7.

A few remarks on poetical composition, and we have 20
done. The art of composition is merely accessory to the
poetical talent. But where that talent exists, it necessarily gives its own character to the style, and renders
it perfectly different from all others. As a poet's habits
of mind lead to contemplation rather than to communi- 25
cation with others, he is more or less obscure according
to the particular style of poetry he has adopted ; less so
in epic, or narrative and dramatic representation, — more
so in odes and choruses. ′ He will be obscure, moreover,

from the depth of his feelings, which require a congenial
reader to enter into them — and from their acuteness,
which shrinks from any formal accuracy in the expression of them.   And he will be obscure, not only from
5 the carelessness of genius, and from the originality of
his conceptions, but it may be from natural deficiency
in the power of clear and eloquent expression, which,
we must repeat, is a talent distinct from poetry, though
often mistaken for it.

10   However, dexterity in composition, or *eloquence* as it
may be called in a contracted sense of the word, is mani-
festly more or less necessary in every branch of literature, though its elements may be different in each.
Poetical eloquence consists, first, in the power of illus-
15 tration ; which the poet uses, not as the orator, volun-
tarily, for the sake of clearness or ornament, but almost
by constraint, as the sole outlet and expression of intense
inward feeling.   This spontaneous power of comparison
may, in some poetical minds, be very feeble ; these of
20 course cannot show to advantage as poets.   Another
talent necessary to composition is the power of unfold-
ing the meaning in an orderly manner.   A poetical
mind is often too impatient to explain itself justly ; it
is overpowered by a rush of emotions, which sometimes
25 want of power, sometimes the indolence of inward enjoyment, prevents it from describing.   Nothing is more
difficult than to analyze the feelings of our own minds ;
and the power of doing so, whether natural or acquired,
is clearly distinct from experiencing them.   Yet, though
30 distinct from the poetical talent, it is obviously necessary
to its exhibition.   Hence it is a common praise bestowed
upon writers, that they express what we have often felt,

but could never describe. The power of arrangement, which is necessary for an extended poem, is a modification of the same talent, being to poetry what method is to logic. Besides these qualifications, poetical composition requires that command of language which is the mere effect of practice. The poet is a compositor; words are his types; he must have them within reach, and in unlimited abundance. Hence the need of careful labor to the accomplished poet, — not in order that his diction may attract, but that the language may be subjected to him. He studies the art of composition as we might learn dancing or elocution; not that we may move or speak according to rule, but that, by the very exercise, our voice and carriage may become so unembarrassed as to allow of our doing what we will with them.

A talent for composition, then, is no essential part of poetry, though indispensable to its exhibition. Hence it would seem that attention to the language, for its own sake, evidences not the true poet, but the mere artist. Pope is said to have tuned our tongue. We certainly owe much to him — his diction is rich, musical, and expressive; still he is not on this account a poet; he elaborated his composition for its own sake. If we give him poetical praise on this account, we may as appropriately bestow it on a tasteful cabinet-maker. This does not forbid us to ascribe the grace of his verse to an inward principle of poetry, which supplied him with archetypes of the beautiful and splendid to work by. But a similar gift must direct the skill of every fancy-artist who subserves the luxuries and elegances of life. On the other hand, though Virgil is celebrated as a

master of composition, yet his style is so identified with
his conceptions, as their outward development, as to pre-
clude the possibility of our viewing the one apart from
the other. ¹ In Milton, again, the harmony of the verse
is but the echo of the inward music which the thoughts
of the poet breathe.   In Moore's style, the ornament
continually outstrips the sense.   Cowper and Walter
Scott, on the other hand, are slovenly in their versifica-
tion.   Sophocles writes, on the whole, without studied
attention to the style ; but Euripides frequently affected
a simplicity and prettiness which exposed him to the ridi-
cule of the comic poets.   Lastly, the style of Homer's
poems is perfect in their particular department.   It is
free, manly, simple, perspicuous, energetic, and varied.
It is the style of one who rhapsodized without deference
to hearer or judge, in an age prior to the temptations
which more or less prevailed over succeeding writers —
before the theatre had degraded poetry into an exhibition, and criticism narrowed it into an art. ``

January, 1829.

NOTE BY THE AUTHOR.

[As printed in the author's *Essays Critical and Historical*, this essay is followed by a note, the subjoined extract from which is especially relevant to the topic discussed.]

The following reference is made to it [the foregoing article] in my "*Religious Opinions*," p. 11 : "I recollect how dissatisfied Dr. Whately was with an article of mine in the *London Review*, which Blanco White good-humoredly only called ' Platonic ' ;" and indeed it certainly omits one of the essential conditions of the idea of Poetry, its relation to the affections, — and that in consequence, as it would seem, of confusing the function and aim of Poetry with its formal object. As the aim of civil government is the well-being of the governed, and its object is expediency ; as the aim of oratory is to persuade, and its object is the probable ; as the function of philosophy is to view all things in their mutual relations, and its object is truth ; and as virtue consists in the observance of the moral law, and its object is the right ; so Poetry may be considered to be the gift of moving the affections through the imagination, and its object to be the beautiful.

I should observe that several sentences of this Essay, which in passing through the press were, by virtue of an editor's just prerogative, altered or changed, now stand as I sent them to him.

NOTES.

1 4. *Aristotle.* *Poetics* 6. 7–9: "All tragedy then must have six parts
. . . : plot, character, sentiment, style, decoration, music. . . . Of these
the most important is the arrangement of incident; for tragedy is a
representation, not of persons, but of action and life, happiness and unhappiness; and happiness and unhappiness consist in action, the end being
action, not a quality."

5 7. *Minute diligence.* Cf. Mahaffy on the *Poetics* (*Hist. Grk. Lit.*
2. 410): "One almost suspects that the author was beginning to disbelieve
in genius, and attribute artistic success to mere soundness and accuracy of
method. How far truer and more appreciative is the tract of Longinus
on the Sublime!"

5 15. *Frequently instanced.* Mahaffy, *Hist. Grk. Lit.* 2. 410: "His
ideal poet seems to have been Sophocles, and his ideal play the Œdipus
Rex."

7 4. "*Quem Deus,*" etc. "Whom a god wishes to destroy, he first
makes mad." A Latin translation of a fragment of Euripides, quoted by
Athenagoras:

Ὅταν δὲ δαίμων ἀνδρὶ πορσύνῃ κακὰ
Τὸν νοῦν ἔβλαψε πρῶτον.

7 21–3. *A Bull,* etc. Euripides, *Bacchæ* 920–2.

8 15. *Pronounces Euripides,* etc. *Poetics* 13. 6: "Euripides, whatever
else he may manage ill, yet appears the most *tragic* of poets."

9 10. "*Without a guide.*" Quoted from Sophocles, *Œdipus at Colonos*
1588.

9 15. "*Decies repetita placebit.*" Horace, *Art of Poetry* 365:

That gives us pleasure for a single view;
And this, *ten times repeated, still is new.*

9 22. *The spectators,* etc. Aristotle, *Poetics* 4. 5.

9 29. *Representation of the ideal.* *Poetics* 9. 1–4; cf. Sidney, *Defense*

31

of Poesy 18 25 ff., Shelley, *Defense of Poetry* 10 9 ff., and the notes on both passages.

10 2. *Phenomenon.* Misprint for "phenomena"?

10 6. *Poesis,* etc. Bacon, *De Augmentis Scientiarum*, Book 2, ch. 13. Compare the similar reflections in his *Advancement of Learning*, 2. 4. 1: "The use of this feigned history hath been to give some shadow of satisfaction to the mind of man in those points wherein the nature of things doth deny it, the world being in proportion inferior to the soul ; by reason whereof there is, agreeable to the spirit of man, a more ample greatness, a more exact goodness, and a more absolute variety, than can be found in the nature of things."

11 10. *Figure is its necessary medium of communication.* Cf. Shelley, *Defense* 4 27 ff.

11 15. *A metrical garb*, etc. Cf. Shelley, *Defense* 8 8 ff.

12 8. *Ninth Iliad.* Probably referring to *Iliad* 9. 449–453.

12 9. *Nurse of Orestes.* Æschylus, *Choephoræ* 736–749.

12 29. *Empedocles.* Cf. Sidney, *Defense* 3 18: "So Thales, Empedocles, and Parmenides sang their natural philosophy in verses."

13 2. *Neither were poets.* Cf. Aristotle, *Poetics* 1. 8: "For if they set forth the principles of medicine or music in metre, people will call them poets, though, except the metre, there is nothing in common between Homer and Empedocles; the one should be called a poet, the other rather a physicist." See also Sidney, *Defense* 9 34—10 11.

14 22. *Brambletye House.* A novel by Horace Smith, published in 1826.

14 26. *Has the fidelity of history.* Chambers' *Cyclopædia of English Literature* says : "Some of its descriptions of the plague in London were copied too literally from Defoe."

14 29. *Incidents.* Printed "Incident" in the *Essays Historical and Critical.*

17 19. *Ladurlad, Thalaba, and Roderick.* Characters respectively of *The Curse of Kehama*, *Thalaba the Destroyer*, and *Roderick, the Last of the Goths.*

18 1. *Old Robin Gray.* By Lady Anne Barnard, d. 6th May, 1825. The ballad was composed about 1771.

18 5. Milman's *Martyr of Antioch*, a closet drama founded on the legend of St. Margaret, was published in 1822 ; Bernard Barton's *Dream* in his *Poems*, 1820.

18 26. "*Sic dicet ille*," etc. Cicero, *Orator* 40. 137 : "He will speak in such a way as to present one and the same thing under different aspects,

and to rest and dwell upon the same thought." The true reading is somewhat different from that in our text : " Sic igitur dicet ille, quem expetimus, ut verset sæpe multis modis eadem et una in re hæreat in eademque commoretur sententia ;" so quoted in Quintilian 9. 1. 41, except that *una* and *in* are transposed.

21 13. *Tityrus's stags.* Alluding to Virgil's *First Eclogue*, 59 : " So first in air the nimble stags shall feed . . . , ere from my heart his look shall pass away."

22 27. *Moral character.* Cf. Shelley, *Defense* 42 33 : " The greatest poets have been men of the most spotless virtue."

23 16. *Partial and limited poetry.* Cf. Shelley, *Defense* 43 4–7.

24 22. *Lucretius.* Cf. Shelley, *Defense* 24 4.

24 25. *Revealed Religion.* Cf. Shelley, *Defense* 5 25 ff., 6 27 ff., 10 8, 14 2 ff., 25 20 ff., 26 13 ff., 27 21 ff., 37 32 ff.

25 29—26 9. *He will be obscure*, etc. It is natural to think of Robert Browning in reading this paragraph.

27 20. *The mere artist.* Is this a prophetic characterization of any living poet ?

28 5. *Echo of the inward music.* Cf. Shelley, *Defense* 9 32 : " Being the echo of the eternal music."

31 20. *Through the imagination.* Cf. Shelley, *Defense* 14 10 ff.

INDEX OF PROPER NAMES.

Æschylus 2 14, 5 23, 7 29.
   Agamemnon 5 9, 23.
   Choephoræ 12 9.
   Prometheus 3 13.
   Thebæ (*Seven against Thebes*)
     3 19.
   See also Antigone, Cassandra,
     Hermes, Nereids, Oceanus,
     Orestes.
Agamemnon 6 2, 18.
Alcestis 3 27.
Antigone 3 4, 21, 32.
Aristotle 1 3, 4, 20, 4 26, 32, 5 11, 8 4,
   26, 9 29, 21 26.

Bacchæ 7 12.
Bacchus 6 26, 7 17.
Bacon 10 6.
Baillie, Joanna 18 8.
Barton, Bernard 18 6.
Brambletye House 14 22.
Burns 23 6.
Byron 12 27, 18 2, 20, 21 2, 16, 24 10.
   Childe Harold 19 9, 21 11.
   Corsair 21 3.
   See also Childe Harold, Myrrha,
     Sardanapalus.

Cadmus 7 9.
Campbell 18 7, 19 7.
Cassandra 6 12.

Charles II. 14 24.
Childe Harold 21 11.
Cicero 18 29.
Clytemnestra 3 27, 16 30.
Cowper 18 3, 23 25, 28 7.
Crabbe 20 5.

Dryden 24 3.

Edgeworth, Miss 14 28, 15 5, 30.
Empedocles 12 29.
Euripides 2 22, 3 26, 7 26, 8 15, 16 31,
   28 10.
   Bacchæ 5 10, 6 25.
   Electra 3 27.
   Hippolytus 3 31.
   Orestes 3 30.
   Phœnissæ 3 32.
   See also Alcestis, Antigone,
     Bacchæ, Bacchus, Cadmus,
     Clytemnestra, Ion, Medea,
     Pentheus, Phædra, Tiresias.

Gibbon 24 20.
Gray 18 9.

Hermes 3 17.
Homer 23 31, 28 12.
   See also Phœnix.
Hume 24 19.

Iago 16 29.
Ion 3 29.

Juvenal 19 22.

Ladurlad 17 19.
Lady Macbeth 17 1.
Lammermoor, Bride of 17 7.
Lucretius 24 22.

Medea 3 28.
Milman 18 4.
Milton 18 5, 10, 23 25, 28 4.
   Il Penseroso 13 12.
   L'Allegro 13 12.
Moore 28 6.
Myrrha 21 23.

Neoptolemus 3 9.
Nereids 3 17.

Oceanus 3 15.
Œdipus 3 4, 5 20, 9 9.
Old Robin Gray 18 1.
Ophelia 17 7.
Oppian 13 1.
Orestes 12 9.

Pentheus 6 27, 7 10.
Phædra 3 30.
Philoctetes 3 10.
Phœnix 12 8.
Polynices 3 5.
Pope 13 22, 27 21.

Richard (III.) 16 28.
Roderick 17 20, 26.
Romeo and Juliet 17 6.
Rousseau 24 20.

Sardanapalus 21 23.
Scott, Walter 14 26, 21 25, 23 29, 28 8·

Ivanhoe 20 32.
Kenilworth 20 31.
Old Mortality 20 32.
Peveril of the Peak 14 22.
Waverley Novels 20 23.
  See also Lammermoor, Bride of.
Shakspeare 12 16, 21 25, 23 30.
   Hamlet 19 30.
   Macbeth 19 30.
   Othello 19 30.
   Richard (III.) 19 30.
  See also Iago, Lady Macbeth,
   Ophelia, Richard, Romeo and
   Juliet.
Sophocles 2 17, 3 2, 7 28, 28 9.
   Ajax 2 19.
   Œdipus at Colonus 2 18, 3 1.
   Œdipus the King 5 10, 14, 28,
    6 24, 8 2, 9 13.
   Philoctetes 2 20, 3 2, 7.
  See also Antigone, Neoptole-
   mus, Œdipus, Philoctetes,
   Polynices, Ulysses.
Southey 17 17, 19, 23 26.
  See also Ladurlad, Roderick,
   Thalaba.
Spenser 23 25.

Thalaba 17 20.
Thomson 13 8.
Tiresias 7 9.
Tityrus 21 13.

Ulysses 3 8.

Virgil 13 22, 24 2, 27 32.
  See also Tityrus.

Wordsworth 23 26.

Young 18 20.

www.ingramcontent.com/pod-product-compliance
Lightning Source LLC
Chambersburg PA
CBHW030908260626
47169CB00008B/2748